I have witnessed the power of Morris. From a young and resti missionary ship, MV LOGOS 1 sense of God's purpose in his li that transformational power. The Gospel that changes lives. This book challenges that longing in you to live a life totally committed to the Lord Jesus Christ.

Lawrence Tong
International Director, Operation Mobilisation

Are you sitting comfortably? Then I'll begin.

Joel is a restless revolutionary, an engineer by background, who gave it all up to help equip the church for a new reformation. This book is his clarion call to the church to go back to its revolutionary roots. Filled with challenges, encouragements, stories and hope, this book will push you deeper into the mission of God.

Are you sitting comfortably? I hope not.

Jonathan Thomas
Pastor of Cornerstone Church, Abergavenny,
and Pastoral Dean of Union School of Theology, Wales

This is a book is a call to spiritual revolution. Each chapter points us to Jesus, the ultimate revolutionary, and shares the testimony of a faithful Christian who lived and 'all in' for Jesus. A short, snappy book that challenges us to go all in for the gospel and reminds us of the power of living a Jesus-centred life.

Mez McConnell
Pastor, Niddrie Community Church, Edinburgh
Director of 20Schemes

REVOLUTIONARY TIONARY GOD

HOW KNOWING HIM CHANGES EVERYTHING

JOEL MORRIS

CHRISTIAN **FOCUS**

Scripture quotations are from *The Holy Bible, English Standard Version*, copyright © 2001 by Crossway Bibles, a publishing ministry of Good News Publishers. Used by permission. All rights reserved. ESV Text Edition: 2011.

Copyright © Joel Morris 2019

paperback ISBN 978-1-5271-0419-8
epub ISBN 978-1-5271-0494-5
mobi ISBN 978-1-5271-0495-2

10 9 8 7 6 5 4 3 2 1

Published in 2019
by
Christian Focus Publications Ltd,
Geanies House, Fearn, Ross-shire,
IV20 1TW, Great Britain.

www.christianfocus.com

Cover by Pete Barnsley (CreativeHoot.com)

Printed and bound
by Bell & Bain, Glasgow

All rights reserved. No part of this publication may be reproduced, stored in a retrieval system, or transmitted, in any form, by any means, electronic, mechanical, photocopying, recording or otherwise without the prior permission of the publisher or a licence permitting restricted copying. In the U.K. such licences are issued by the Copyright Licensing Agency, Saffron House, 6-10 Kirby Street, London, EC1 8TS www.cla.co.uk

Contents

Foreword 7

Introduction 9

1. Personal Revolution 13
2. Radical Union 21
3. Revolutionary Truth 33
4. Vive La Revolution 47
5. The Father of Revolutions 61

Conclusion 73

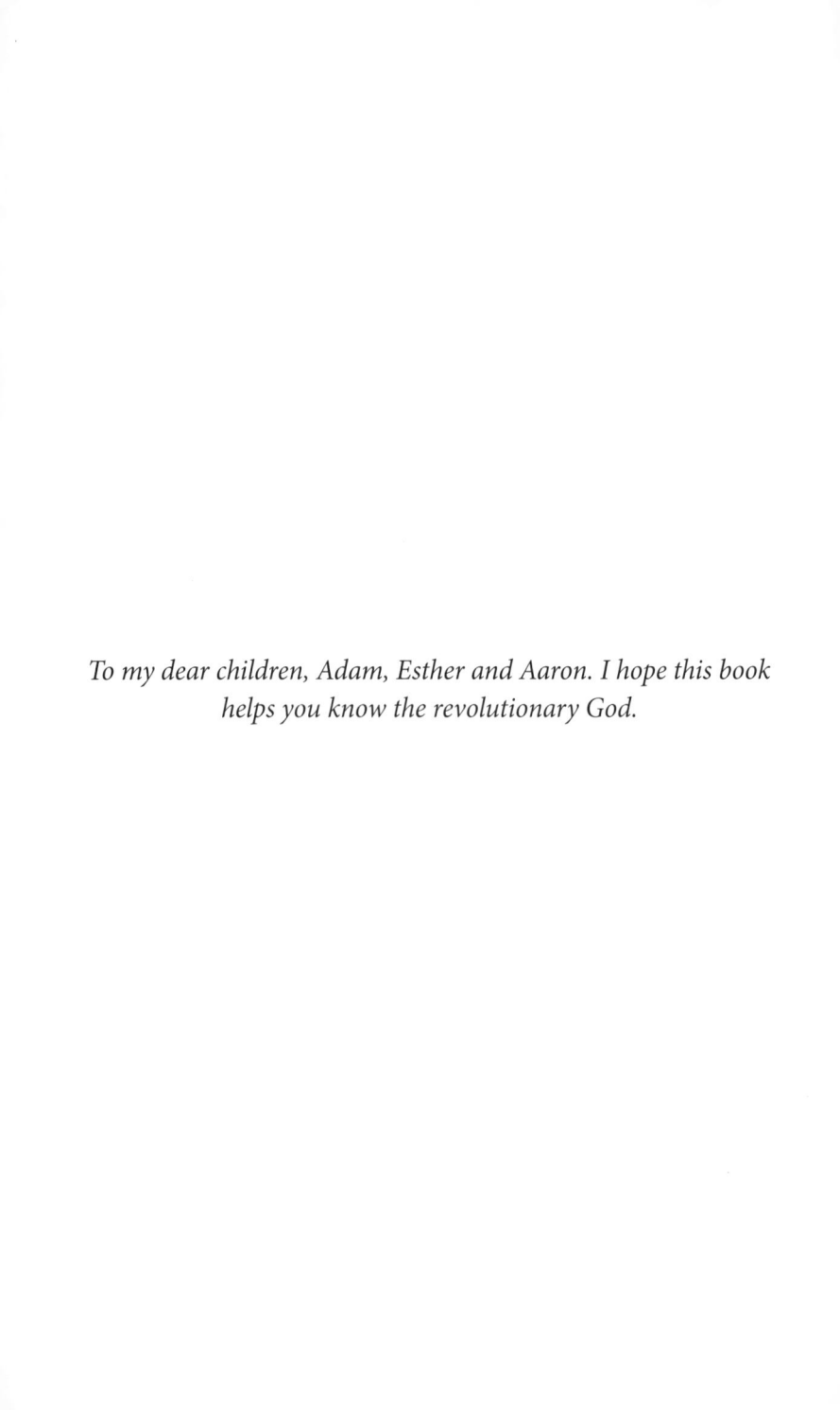

To my dear children, Adam, Esther and Aaron. I hope this book helps you know the revolutionary God.

Foreword

The Christian gospel is not an 'add-on' to an otherwise well-functioning life. The gospel brings an utter re-orientation, a new life entirely – the Bible says it is nothing short of resurrection, a new existence that goes against the flow of everything around us in the world. In other words, it is a matter of revolution.

Joel Morris understands this. He has travelled the world extensively and has seen the revolutionary nature of authentic Christianity. And God has given him a burden to see a re-igniting of spiritual revolution once more in his native Europe.

Revolutionary God takes us deep into the heart of the Christian gospel and reminds us of its incendiary truths – the endless love of the revolutionary Himself Jesus Christ, dying and rising again for our gracious rescue; the vital but neglected importance of Christian unity; the preciousness of clear doctrine; and the all-or-nothing response that the gospel demands.

Deeply inspiring are the portraits in each chapter of great Christians from the past – great not on their own steam, of course, but simply sincere in their trust in God and therefore history-altering in their divinely given significance. But throughout the focus is not centrally on any magnificent Christian but on a magnificent Christ, limitless in grace and bracing in His call, who beckons to us in the twenty-first century to lay down all that distracts or frightens us for the sake of participating in the greatest revolution of all time – the advance of the kingdom of God through its crucified and risen King.

Dane Ortlund

Senior Vice President for Bible Publishing, Crossway

Introduction

We like underdogs, don't we? We love to see them win against all odds. A football side coming from far behind to win, or a talent show underdog making the final. A ragtag rebellion massively outgunned overthrowing an oppressive regime. They make movies about it. It never gets old. We like to think that ordinary people can achieve something extraordinary, even change the world. Maybe while growing up, you were a follower of a rock band or political group? It seems people like to belong to something a little bit dangerous, perhaps a bit subversive and out of the mainstream. It's a curious thing, yet many of us will relate to this attraction to the outsider or the underdog. Revolution can be a dangerous thing. Maybe you can remember a time in your life when revolution was in the air? When anything was possible, it was all in flux, and new horizons seemed to open up before you.

Well, history is absolutely full of revolutions. Revolutions are movements that need revolutionaries to lead them. People who will stand up against oppression, who will lead a movement, and who embody the very heart values of the movement. The heart of the revolutionary is passionate and committed, it's about being all in. That's what other people buy into: a movement with a leader who's the real deal. Such a movement is exciting, moving and winsome. It ignites people's hearts. The revolutionary's message is compelling, something people can strongly relate to and get behind. Sharing from their heart to the heart of the people, inspiring belief in the vision and mission of the movement. So that people throw themselves behind them and give their energy, passion and resources for the cause. However, revolutions don't go on forever and usually die out with their founders. The hopes and dreams of a generation, gone and dashed. Dreams of lasting freedom, a better life and brighter future for the poor and needy have faded away. These are merely shadows of the true revolution.

There is someone who was sent to save the world. He was the only answer, that's how bad things were. He came to bring freedom to the captives and liberty to the oppressed. All the Bible stories promising a saviour were true! Here was a freedom fighter and revolutionary, an outsider stepping in, just as God had promised from the beginning. He had such humble beginnings in this world. He was not someone who you'd think would make a difference. This was born out of His selfless love. He was like light flooding into a pitch-black room, and hope suddenly broke through.

Unlike other revolutionaries, Jesus wasn't a political or a military leader, but He did come to bring the greatest revolution to humanity. First, to the nation where He was born, and from there it spread out all over the world. Today His movement numbers in the billions and is still gaining in strength. But

Introduction

never before in the history of the world has there been such fierce opposition to His revolution. Continuing bloodshed and violence are endured every day by His followers. Yet His revolution prevails, and no one can stop it. It will go on and on, until He returns.

Revolutions tend to affect a country's culture, economy, and socio-political structures, and many, many have erupted over the centuries. All have something in common. They are usually movements that unite people, as they revolt against an oppressive political or social structure. The revolution we have been describing doesn't primarily affect those three factors (although, you could argue it might have these consequences eventually). It is, first and foremost, a movement of the heart. It's described by its leader as a revolution of the heart and mind – a revolution of the whole person, from the inside out.

You might not think of yourself as having taken part in any revolution but, if you are someone who would identify as a follower of Jesus Christ, then you certainly have done and are doing! Here's a man who healed the sick and raised the dead. He defied an evil empire and found time for the weakest and most vulnerable. He was the one sent to save the world from the ultimate oppressive regime. He brought the biggest change to the ancient world and to humanity forever. What He did nearly two thousand years ago will never cease to be felt and experienced. The shockwaves of the arrival of this revolutionary still shake the world today.

Now, if you believe and trust that Jesus is God's only-begotten, eternal Son, sent by God the Father through the Holy Spirit to become a man, to save us from the slavery of our sins... If you believe that He died a martyr's death on the cross and was resurrected from the dead after three days... If you believe that He now reigns supreme over all things at the right hand of His Father mediating for those who follow after Him... If you believe He is the way, the truth and the life for all people... then you believe in the greatest revolutionary of all time.

For His fellow-revolutionaries, Jesus has paid the greatest price. If all this really is true and trustworthy, then this is the most incendiary and divisive message you will ever hear or speak about. You could certainly lose your life for it. It brings confrontation to a world set in its ways, denying and hating the very existence of a loving creator God. The world will always try to dumb down and kill off this radical Jesus and His zealots. Unfortunately, no revolution is without some bloodshed. The world is at odds with its creator who makes all things new.

1.
Personal Revolution

'Do not be conformed to this world, but be transformed by the renewal of your mind, that by testing you may discern what is the will of God, what is good and acceptable and perfect.' (Rom. 12:2)

As people, we change along our journey through life. We grow in our bodies but also in our emotions and in our minds. Even more so, those who follow Jesus are people who grow. Transforming from darkness and spiritual poverty, to light and the riches of God. It's quite a metamorphosis. Though we don't look any different on the outside physically, there's an internal change, a heart and mind thing. Our attitudes change, being shaped by the almighty God. This fruit can certainly be seen by those who really know us.

It is clear from Paul's letter to the church in Rome that, for those who have turned to Jesus, their minds are constantly being renewed by the Word of God (the truth) and by the Spirit of God. Fossilisation isn't part of God's plan for us as His new creations. Fossilisation is for dead things, but Christ is life and growth. So, we need to be careful of falling into the trap of thinking, 'I'm now a good Christian, so I can sit back and wait for heaven'. No, we need ongoing personal revolution. As long as we're alive on this earth, we will struggle against the sinful flesh (our rebellious nature) within and the devil without. So we need regular renewal in God. Christ is the source of our life, and we need to keep tapping the spring of life.

The Bible teaches a lot about people. It says that people who are without Christ have a fallen nature, and are separated from God. In his letter to the Roman church, the Apostle Paul describes people without Christ as being given over by God to dishonourable passions. They worship the creature rather than the creator (Rom. 1:24-5), whether they know this or not. But, those who believe and trust in Jesus, while still having the old broken nature, now also have the new life-giving nature of Jesus, which fights against and works to reform the other. Again and again, it is important that there is a breaking of the bonds that try to ensnare us, and from which the power of Christ continually frees us. We are saved to be free and to stay living free! This is revolution.

The problem is that we tend to minimise how big a problem sin is for us, and our minds are drawn back to conformity with the world we live in. We are repeat offenders who need continual rehabilitation. We need daily refreshment through reading the Bible and through prayer, meeting with other Christians in Bible study and corporate worship. We need to fill our minds and hearts with passion for the things of God. Fossilisation is easier and it takes no energy, but reforming takes work! It takes constant work, a labour of love. It also takes support from others. We need accountability from more mature Christians, especially those in church leadership. Yet this is a non-negotiable, for we've tasted such a personal reformation,

NOT SETTLING FOR WHAT YOU KNOW

I grew up in the green countryside of South Wales, in a place affectionately known as 'The Valleys'. It was known for stone chapels, revivals, coal mines, heavy industry and male voice choirs. For better or worse, the main source of employment was effectively removed during the 1980s. The mines and many factories seemed to close overnight, and, for many, life became very hard.

A disused colliery in Rhondda

To see the rapid decline of one's society and experience personal poverty in your formative years does something to your character and personality. Though I never went hungry, my father struggled to find work at times. Many fathers struggled to find work and provide for their families. It's strange how the decline in the church matched the decline of the economy and society. It was a place where childhood friends growing up had no hope for a bright future and many turned down dark alleyways to use drugs and alcohol to numb that reality. Some friends I grew up with ended up in prison or worse.

I grew up gazing at the horizon, longing to escape to something more. I longed to explore the big wide world outside my valley. I could never have imagined to what extent I would travel. Indeed, God has been so good to me. In the end, I didn't run away. Instead, I was called away to the mission field with Operation Mobilisation (OM). But I remember being dis-satisfied with the lack of vision in the local church and of feeling stunted in my own spiritual growth. I grew up in a church whose mission was to coal miners. I had been warmed there by the Holy Spirit and by stories of revival, but we were looking to the past. I wanted to grow and experience the triune God of the Bible who did miracles and to get to know the immense power of His Word to change lives today.

My story will resonate with many I'm sure. After decades of decline in the United Kingdom and continental Europe, the Church is thankfully experiencing a small resurgence through church-planting and church-rejuvenation work. We have recently celebrated 500 years of Reformation or the 'revolution in the medieval Catholic Church', and Europe is still in dire need of new reformation, just as it was all those years ago. There are fairly similar challenges and problems facing the Protestant Church and more so the Roman Catholic and Orthodox Churches. The Reformation was about purifying the Church, to get back to the true teaching of Jesus and the Word of God. It's a reminder that the Church – God's revolutionary force – needs a revolution when it goes to seed. Unfortunately, it happens all too often!

It does seem that God prunes His Church by letting some churches die off. Then He brings new growth through planting movements for effective new churches to flourish. Some existing churches are rejuvenated and there is growth once again where before there was decline. God doesn't stand still. He is revolutionary. But godly leaders still need to be raised up and gospel-hearted churches must be established which will preach the gospel and make disciples. We mustn't settle for what we know but seek gospel growth in our lives and churches.

SO WHY TALK OF REVOLUTION?

The world you live in, created by God, has been subverted by the god of this world, the Devil, and is under a curse. The world is, in fact, rigged! You are either going along with this subversion and are under the curse, or you are part of the revolution set on spreading the word of God to rescue people for Jesus. This truth is dangerous, its message will kill you. It will take you as a sinner and deliver you into Christ's death. But, God will raise you up as a new person. Why care about the revolution? Because the revolution is from God to save us for His glory and for our joy.

So, how does a new person in Christ make sense of this world in order to know how to live? Where do we get our bearings, now that we no longer belong? If the world around us has been overthrown, we need a different compass to make the right decisions. We can't trust the world – our news and data are fake. Only knowledge of God's Word and the Holy Spirit living in us enable our minds to test what is good for us, and what is the will of God for our lives.

This makes sense if the Bible teaches us about the source of absolute truth, God Himself. With this knowledge, the Holy Spirit helps us to know the will of God for us so we can lead godly lives, making choices to grow in knowledge of God and not grow in patterns of sin which lead to death, choices to keep reforming and purifying. Knowing God, our hearts and minds are shaped to go after the things of God, leading us into His free gift of eternal life.

Our transformation from darkness to light is a journey, a process making us like the one we're following who is the light of the world. In the Church we call this process discipleship. The church also, like the mind, needs to be renewed or reformed from time to time. It means acknowledging our fallen state, that we are not perfect and sinless in ourselves and have been and are being saved and set apart for God; being made holy unto the holy God. It is important then that we as people are contrite of heart and are continually reforming our minds to fight the good fight against snares and forces that pull us back – that we keep throwing them off! We have been set free from our slavery for freedom (Gal. 5:1). We must stand firm and not allow ourselves to become enslaved again.

» John Newton

John Newton was a captain of a slave ship. We think of these people today as the lowest of the low, and John Newton certainly had this reputation. He was the most hard, crass and immoral man you could meet. He was quite the toilet mouth and enjoyed blaspheming. In his own words, 'I was exceedingly vile'[1]. I'm not sure if I know anyone like this now, but I think I've met a few in my travels.

John Newton (1725–1807)

---

1   Aitken, J. *John Newton: From disgrace to amazing grace* (Wheaton IL: Crossway, 2007), preface.

Personal Revolution

Modern-day comparisons might be those heartless exploiters sending hundreds of desperate refugees across the Mediterranean Sea in boats that should have been condemned a long time ago. Taking the only money hopeless people have for a seat to the watery depths. Or we could compare him to a big-time drug dealer making a fortune on the lives of others, seeking to keep those addicts in slavery and misery until their death. This paints a pretty damning picture of the man. He was a pretty despicable character, but God had a plan for John.

On a voyage aboard a cargo ship returning home from West Africa where he had plumbed the depths of depravity and witchcraft, John met the almighty God in a storm. After reading a book about Jesus which he found on board, he gently fell asleep only to awake to a roaring storm. Fearing for his life, and finding that the rotten ship beneath him was filling with cold seawater, he attempted to navigate safely the wild black chaos of the stormy sea, and he found that God wasn't far away. Where would his soul go if he went down with the ship?

To his own great surprise, Newton prayed to God for mercy. It was in that moment of turning that John Newton underwent a personal revolution that had an immediate effect. He stopped swearing and changed his riotous behaviour, a sign that he had met with the revolutionary and living God. He began reading the Bible and praying every day. He still had his many struggles. He went back to sea as a captain of slave ships. He had changed, but his job hadn't. Eventually, ill health took him from the sea to work on land.

Later in his life John became terribly sorry for his career and repentant about the things he had done. God had set him on a very different path from the one he had been on. No longer was he on a path towards death, but to life. In his famous hymn

'Amazing Grace', John captures the miracle of new life in Jesus, 'I once was lost, but now I'm found, was blind but now I see.' John the outcast was found and overturned by a gracious and loving God. He was welcomed into a family, the people of God. He discovered wonderful union with Christ and His people. John's story shows us that the Christian life is not one of don'ts and duty, but of personal revolution and growth.

2.
Radical Union

In the previous chapter, I touched upon the Reformation and the revolution that happened within the Roman Catholic Church. At the time, this was the state religion of the Holy Roman Empire (Roman Catholic Europe). The Reformation was a tremendous earthquake that shook the foundations of Europe. The Reformers were kicked out of the church, persecuted and many were martyred. On coming out of the state church, the Reformers could easily have opted for a more individualistic way of church. They had been disillusioned with the state church and could have argued that union and submission to authority is no good.

However, contrary to our kind of modern individualism that tells us that it's all about our own personal experience of God, the Reformers weren't radical individualists who couldn't conform to church authority. Martin Luther actually did not want to leave the church, he wanted to reform it from the inside, but was pushed out because of the threat he posed to the Pope and the business of the church. The business of the church was to keep people in darkness and slavery, and to keep extracting money from the people who didn't know any better. So, a revolution was called for, for the sake of the church. Luther was a prophet sent by God to reform His church, calling her back to the faith of the gospel.

Our personal revolution calls each of us to be collectively one in Christ to fight for Him. It means to turn away from worldly individualistic self-gratification to a gathered vibrant community of believers, sacrificially working to lift up its head, who is Jesus! Here's where we, as the Lord's gathered, called-out people, come together in union with Jesus, but now against the world that doesn't know Him who made it. We are a revolutionary army, at war with the Devil, and he with us. Looking to strike at any moment, he is constantly attacking the church around the world through his powers and principalities. But, like an army that has a mission and organisation, so the Church of Christ moves as one to carry out its great objective. Our weapon is the Word of God. Our spiritual armour shields us from the fiery missiles of the evil one, who is set on killing us. Our warfare is a spiritual one. And we are most effective when we fight together, in unity through Jesus our head who is our awesome power and stronghold. If we become isolated and alone, we can be easily overcome. Union is essential to survive and grow as a Christian.

A BIBLICAL PICTURE OF UNION

A useful image from the Old Testament to help us understand biblical union is found in Psalm 133. Israel's High Priest is anointed with oil, and this is a wonderful picture of the love and union of the Trinity – the Father pouring out the Holy Spirit on the Son who is the anointed one. In the Psalm, the precious oil represents the Spirit and Jesus having the name of Christ (anointed) is called our Great High Priest. If not so, then this is a very confusing Psalm. Why would pouring oil on to the head of the priest be like unity for the church unless there was a deeper meaning?

Thousands of years ago the High Priest was the person from the tribe of priests in the nation of Israel who mediated between God and His people. He had special ceremonial clothes to wear and various cleansing and sacrificial rituals to perform in the temple. As the priest carried the ephod (a breastplate) over his shoulders and chest, this represented the twelve tribes, and so Jesus our High Priest carries the church on His body. He carries the church on His heart and shoulders, and with the oil of anointing poured down on the head, flowing on to His body, so people of God truly are part of the High Priest. The love of God flows down from the Father to His Son and on to His church by the Spirit of God.

Psalm 133 illustrates how God's people would sing this amazing truth. See that there's true blessing in unity – because they are united in Christ the blessing comes through Him, down from our head:

Behold, how good and pleasant it is
when brothers dwell in unity!
It is like the precious oil on the head,
running down on the beard,
on the beard of Aaron,
running down on the collar of his
  robes!

A Painting of the High Priest

It is like the dew of Hermon,
which falls on the mountains of Zion!
For there the Lord has commanded the blessing,
life for evermore.

The Bible teaches that God has anointed His church in Christ: '*And it is God who establishes us with you in Christ, and has anointed us, and who has also put his seal on us and given us his Spirit in our hearts as a guarantee*' (2 Cor. 1:21-2).

Through our union with Christ, the Holy Spirit poured on Christ is poured out in our hearts. This is the sweet blessing of this union, the Spirit flows down from the Father on to the Son, who is our head, and on to His body the church. The love of God poured on us from the Father through the Son. So, blessing comes through unity in the church in union with Christ its head. Therefore, it's obvious why there's an emphasis in the New Testament on Christians meeting together and not neglecting to gather. We are created to be in community with each other and with God.

What does it mean if we don't gather together regularly for singing, prayer, preaching of the word, communion and fellowship? That we're not really in union with a body of believers? Believers are called to be gathered together in Christ, and so to resist this unity of the body is to miss out on the blessing this union brings. It is to resist the gathering, the headship of Christ and the authority of the church. Tragically, they miss out on the shaping and formation of discipleship and mentoring, and will not grow very well. They will become deficient with regards to the building up of the word in love and the experience of the Holy Spirit. They miss out on the sacraments – baptism and communion are signs and seals of participation in Christ. They are missing out on everything it means to be a Christian. This is a great sadness.

Let's think for a moment about those who want to sow discord and disunity in church. It's a murderous thing to try to separate the head from the body and the members from the body. Think about the biblical picture of union! Colossians 2:19-23 says that we are to hold fast to the head, that is Christ and His truth! This is clearly a warning to the church that there are forces at work to kill our union. The Reformers were not murderers. They were working for union in Christ, but not under the Pope or the Priest.

False teaching can have the appearance of wisdom in promoting self-made religion, asceticism and severity to our bodies, but is completely useless in combating sin. Religious showiness that makes you feel 'something spiritual' is merely a fake when compared to knowing the authentic Christ. This is what the Reformers were fighting against in the Roman Catholic Church. And so, reformation draws us back to the source truth of Christ, so we can hold fast to Him. The reforming of our minds continually focuses our hearts together to Jesus. Our hearts are not divorced from our minds and so the reformed mind yields a healthy God-loving heart.

Martin Luther, in his 'monastery tower experience' had a reformation of heart and mind by the grace brought to him when he first saw Christ. Not as a vengeful righteous judge but as the merciful saviour who justifies us by His own righteousness. Understanding with the mind and believing with the heart, he simply receives the gift.

Luther proclaimed a revolutionary message that would set off a chain reaction to reform the church and change the world. But, Luther didn't sit back and say, *I'm saved now I can rest easy*. He launched himself into writing a great many volumes of weighty books to begin unleashing the word of God. He kept writing and pushing, reforming his thinking, reforming the church and dialoguing with people like Erasmus. He was prolific in writings that communicated knowledge about God, a commentary on the Bible and the gospel message. What a fellow-revolutionary. A fellow-heir with Christ.

He lived a liberated life in Jesus. Living out his theology (his knowledge of God) which warmed his heart. He inflamed others around him with the fire of the gospel. Gathering to enjoy his wife's home-made brew, they talked about God and the Bible till the wee small hours. Luther's love for this gracious and radically loving God overflows through every facet.

PURSUING JOYOUS UNION

By continually reforming ourselves by applying the Word of God, we put off the old self; we die to ourselves but are alive to Christ. Then, with our hearts pursuing the source of joy and satisfaction together, all our needs are supplied in Him. As we are in Jesus through the Spirit, we share in all the riches of His Father. Now we are pilgrims in the world, set apart from it. So, our needs and joy don't flow from it anymore. Joy is instead multiplied in our union together with Him. So, why would you deprive yourself of such a joy? It is like the dew of Hermon!

Being radical nowadays can mean that we are being separatist. *I'm doing my own thing because I can't agree with anyone else and don't have the patience to be with them.* However, being radical and a reformer shouldn't be angular and ungracious Christianity. In Genesis 1, God said, *'Let us make man in our image'*. The Godhead united as one and life flows from them in creation. God is forever triune. God then said, it's not good for man to be alone, without union of his own kind. So, Eve was created from Adam. God made marriage as a joyous union that is a reflection of the Trinity and shall not be separated. Joy is multiplied in union.

This concept of union contradicts the idea of the zealous radical, who is too quick to break fellowship and unwilling to submit to church authority. Sadly, I'm sure we can think of examples in the western church today, where there is a culture of independence. 'I'm off to go it alone, God has told me to do this….'. Again, this is not what the Reformers did. As Luther's understanding of Christ and His righteousness was reformed, he and others were forced to leave the church they were trying to reform. Where the union with Christ is breaking down, as we can see with some of the seven churches in the beginning of the book of Revelation, God speaks and calls His church back into union with its head, just as He did through Luther and Calvin.

Our Christian life means practically being one with Christ – as He gathers you to Himself, He's gathered others with you. We have to love those because they're also in Christ. So, when it comes to reforming others it must always be done through grace and love. We know this because of the love we see in the triune God. The Father eternally loves His Son, and so we love the Son through the Spirit[1]. True reformation of the church is loving and gracious, and yet still a godly revolutionary movement. Those who are being used by the Spirit to call the body back to the word of God are to be cherished and embraced, not attacked. The reformed mind wants to reform others, it is a discipleship instinct driven by love for God and His church.

---

1   Reeves, M. *The Good God: Enjoying Father, Son and Spirit* (Milton Keynes: Paternoster, 2012), p. 97.

Union with Christ means solidarity for the faith of the gospel as described in Philippians 1:27. Standing firm for the faith of the gospel means our minds aligned to one cause. If we are standing together for the gospel we cannot fossilise, drifting off to a quiet slumber. The conflict will come to engulf us as it did the Apostle Paul who challenges the Philippian church not to fear the world but to stand, to act, to fight against spiritual darkness and even Satan himself. But, how can we stand? It's clear from the Bible that our lives need to be united around the gospel of Christ, to be one in spirit and mind. We are interdependent with each other, we need each other so the body can grow. This kind of radical union brings sure joy in the midst of the tumult of battle, but the same is not true if we become isolated from other Christians.

Thinking about our own times, in Europe today, we need more gospel unity in the Protestant church. There is too much politics, tribalism and protection of doctrine etc. We need to work for unity among those who hold to this revolutionary Reformation view of God, drawing together from across denominations, networks and tribes within the church. However, this must not be at the cost of holding firm to the truth, uniting around Christ, His word and gospel. It must lead to a revival in our churches and grace-filled revolution in the streets! We long to see Europe truly won back for Christ once more from secularism and paganism.

» George Verwer

When I think of modern revolutionaries who have made an impact on society in the last fifty years, and on the global church and its mission, George Verwer has to be one of the most significant. George is someone whom God has used to

George Verwer (born 1938)

reform His Church around the world. Whatever people think of him, it is clear to see that he has had a big impact on millions of people, either directly or indirectly. He is someone who is all-in. A firebrand. And, as someone who has served in Operation Mobilisation (the missions agency that he set up), I have met him on numerous occasions and looked up to him as a role model and a leader. He has an amazing memory for people, and this comes in handy when he prays for the thousands he meets and gets to know. A humble and teachable leader who cares, he writes thousands of caring letters and emails to those God brings to his mind. He has written, published and distributed many Christian books, mainly on mission and evangelism.

His quotes are famous throughout OM. This one is particularly suitable for this context:

> *We seem to have a strange idea of Christian service. We will buy books, travel miles to hear a speaker on blessings, pay large sums to hear a group singing the latest Christian songs - but we forget that we are soldiers.*[2]

Meaning that Christian service means suffering since we are engaged in a spiritual battle against the prince of this world. The Christian life is revolution against the order of 'the world',

---

2   Verwer, G. *Global Passion* (OM Books, 2014), p. 61.

and is at odds with it. Following Jesus brings us inevitably into conflict and suffering because of Christ. We suffer with Christ because we are united in Him, partaking in His sufferings and are soldiers for Him! We're not to be as we once were – at home in the world we were born into.

Growing up, George was a brash high school kid who had struggles with lust and anger, it's a familiar story for many I'm sure. I can certainly relate. He got into fights and even formed a little gang. You can just imagine this in New Jersey in the 1950s, New York having become one of the world's greatest cities following the war. In 1955, George was wonderfully saved under the evangelism ministry of Billy Graham. A few years later when he was eighteen, he had a job selling fire extinguishers door-to-door around New Jersey, which moved on to selling Bibles and Christian books. Then he started a mission called 'Send the Light' almost sixty years ago, funded by his hard-earned book sales. This took him initially to Mexico, and then later when he moved into Europe, it became Operation Mobilisation.

OM was said to be the first mission agency to champion short-term mission and pioneer the ship ministries of *Logos*, *Doulos* and *Logos Hope* which have brought the gospel to millions of people around the world. This ministry has also helped to raise up Christian leaders in churches around the world and in the marketplace.

God used George to bring a revolution to global missions, a man on fire to see people saved. George's plea is still 'global mission and evangelism at any cost, so that all peoples would have the gospel'. His passion is for all peoples to get to know and love the God of the Bible. George has made his fair share of mistakes, but is humble enough to accept and learn from them. This is what he calls Messiology, how God works through our sin and mess for His glory. He won't be remembered as a theological giant, but a giant of faith, a mobiliser for the church to carry out her great commission. George shows us that we must be the same as our revolutionary God. Standing together in radical union as the Church for the gospel means revolution for the world.

3.
Revolutionary Truth

I wonder, how has your view of God been shaped? If it is by something other than the Bible, then logic dictates that you don't know the God of the Bible. That makes sense, doesn't it? How would you know this God of the Bible without reading it? How can we be like Him if we don't really know Him? He has chosen to reveal Himself through His word, and it is read and preached throughout the world by messengers He has called to do this. If you think you know this God from your own imagination, it is only a vague idea of god or a mouldable god that you fit to what suits you, depending on how you feel. Maybe it's a genie god who you go to when you need something? Well, this isn't the covenantal God of Abraham, Isaac and Jacob, whom the patriarchs of Israel found in the Old Testament (the Bible). This same God is proclaimed by the Apostle Peter at the Beautiful Gate at the Temple in Jerusalem, found in Acts 3:13-15:

> *The God of Abraham, the God of Isaac, and the God of Jacob, the God of our fathers, glorified his servant Jesus, whom you delivered*

over and denied in the presence of Pilate, when he had decided to release him. But you denied the Holy and Righteous One, and asked for a murderer to be granted to you, and you killed the Author of life, whom God raised from the dead. To this we are witnesses.

This, the covenantal God of the Jews, sent His servant to satisfy and reform the old covenant into the new. But, since the God of Abraham, Isaac and Jacob was the one who sent Jesus, the revolutionary Jesus is utterly orthodox. He fulfils the law and the prophetic writing found in the Old Testament by presenting Himself as the lamb to be slain for the world. Biblical reformation draws us closer to the God of the Bible and the truth, and away from the world. It's not rebellion for rebellion's sake. Through reforming the covenant, Jesus makes the God of the Bible known to His people Israel, and to the world.

So, if Jesus makes God known, we must shape our knowledge of God and His world from the source of truth, His word. It was, and still is, a revolutionary and dangerous truth, but at the same time it is utterly orthodox. Orthodoxy is simply the traditional or generally accepted beliefs held by devout believers of a religion or philosophy. In the Protestant Christian's case, these orthodox beliefs are at odds with a world in rebellion against God and His obedient servant who created it. This is a high view of God and the church, not humanising God into our neat little view of the world. But, it is also not angular and separatist, all about protecting doctrinal purity. It is confident and generous like the Reformers, keen to share the revolution with those who need to hear.

Let's take a look at one of those Reformers, John Calvin of Geneva. Calvin was confident in God's sovereignty, and in his theological writings he championed this because he wanted people to see and understand how awesome and glorious the God of the Bible is. This truth enabled people to love and fear God more and surrender under His mighty hand. Calvin didn't mean people to just accept the world and everything as set and unchangeable, or to stop trying to reach people with the gospel. God is absolutely sovereign, but He didn't create mindless robots. This is obvious from the beginning with the creation covenant between God and Adam. Adam obviously had free will to break the covenant.

John Calvin (1509–1564)

Actually, this knowledge of God breeds revolutionaries just like John Calvin and Martin Luther. They are not revolting against God but are becoming like their revolutionary God through Jesus. To have this reformation understanding of God (theology), affects our view of the world and our place in it. It means being ready to answer the Father's call to risk all for Christ and His free gift of righteousness. It's a mind-set that isn't satisfied with the world and quite often the state of the church. But, it is a mind-set that still strives for unity around an orthodox and biblical understanding of God.

THE HEART OF THE REVOLUTIONARY

It is tempting to think that Calvin and Luther were hard-core risk takers, but that's not what their writings say. The Christian revolutionary has a large heart full of the love and fear of almighty God. It is warmed by the fuel of the gospel burning deep down – this is a deep spiritual revolution! This kind of heart is the engine of the revolution, which starts deep within and works itself out. Christ is all in, for His mission – when He was glorified on the cross. We Christians reflect Christ's heart, following after Him through death to resurrection. We are all in, like Jesus who has gone ahead. When you see, believe, fear and love the Father through the Son, you will be 'all in'! Trusting that God has the best plan for your life, you'll say, 'Whatever it takes, I'm all in!' We need to realise that God has the best plan to glorify Himself through the local church, and so the logical response from the church is 'we're all in!' The gospel sparks an unquenchable flame in our hearts, so are we willing to burn for it as did some of the English Reformers martyred for holding to this orthodox understanding of the word of God?

Jesus, who is revolutionary in every sense, while on earth was an exile and a sojourner. He was despised and rejected by His own people. He was acquainted with grief, suffering much, yet He was not embittered. This makes Him a great doctor to other exiles, binding up the broken-hearted, curing all manner of diseases of the heart. Matthew 12:20 describes the heart of Jesus in the midst of persecution by the religious rulers of Jerusalem seeking His immediate death:

a bruised reed he will not break, and a smouldering wick he will not quench.

He came to His own, and His own didn't receive Him. He was handed over and denied. He was an exile, yet He enjoyed the community of the Trinity at all times. Jesus is love because of God's fatherly love poured out on Him and us. 1 Peter 1 says that Christians are to live as exiles in the world like Jesus, and enjoy community as gathered people through union with the Son, through the Spirit and in the Father. We will suffer as exiles, but we reflect His heart; large hearts to love through suffering. That's what people buy. It's the real deal. The heart-warming, winsome, grace-filled gospel bringing the affectionate love of God to the world through the Son.

THE WORD IS OUR LIGHT

Athanasius, Bishop of Alexandria in Egypt in the fourth century, asked who else could bring this grace and love of the Father? 'Who else but the Word of God himself, who also in

Athanasius banished from Alexandria

the beginning had made all things out of nothing?'[1] Christ alone could give us the right to become children of God – rather than punishing us as we deserved, He brings us to God. In John 1, we read that the Word came to bring the light. To do a specific illumination task just like the famous lighthouse in Alexandria, which was one of the seven wonders of the world, shone brightly into the darkness of the Nile. This true light is life itself as the author of creation, and He fills all things. He was with God in the beginning, speaking the world into being out of nothing. Then He came to reform all, bringing the light of the glory of God, to suffer and die on the cross and then mediate for us with the Father.

This was the reason the Word of God entered our world and became flesh, the immortal put on mortality. Athanasius makes the point that 'he was not far from it before, for no part of creation had ever been without him. Who, while ever abiding in union with the Father, yet fills all things that are.'[2] But now He entered the world in a new way as the Son of man, humbling Himself as a servant, the self-revealing Word of God to us. He lived among people, He brought grace and truth, making God known. And is true God from true God.

But, there's constant resistance to the light revolution because people in their natural state love darkness and shun the light. The net effect was that His own didn't receive Him, they wouldn't receive the truth even contending that they were guarding the truth. Jesus the eternal Word of God was rejected as a baby and rejected as a king. He was a man of sorrows, despised and rejected. He didn't come to get along with the

---

1   Athanasius, *On the Incarnation*, pp. 7-8

2   Ibid.

Revolutionary Truth

world, He came to confront the world with words and lead a revolution.

Romans 9:33 says, *'Behold, I am laying in Zion a stone of stumbling, and a rock of offense; and whoever believes in him will not be put to shame.'*

The consequence of this light coming into the world is that the revolutionary Jesus either causes offence or joy. Many have met Him and rejected His message because of the offence. Jesus caused offence to His own people because He proclaimed the true word of God. But, to a few who believed by faith, they followed Him and gained eternal life. Nowhere has the struggle between light and darkness been so acutely seen, yet the only blood shed was His own. Given for those who didn't even know Him, to make them righteous. The light shines in the darkness and the light always wins!

The struggle between light and darkness still continues. Christians are despised and rejected, we are exiles just like Jesus. What does darkness do to stop the growth of the church? It does what it did to Christ, it seeks to kill the life-giving word. The gospel. For hundreds of years, people were in darkness in Europe without access to the word of God. But, the Reformation saw the word of God coming back into the hands of the people, not just for the priests to bend and twist for their own money-making schemes. Luther's translation of the Bible into the people's language and the development of the Gutenberg Press brought mass production to make the word of God accessible for the masses. Light broke through into the darkness! This development later influenced the translation of the English Bible by William Tyndale who also took advantage of the new printing technology.

The Reformers were real entrepreneurs, this comes through in the historical accounts of Luther with his publishing machine and Calvin with an extraordinary missionary strategy transforming France. This speaks of the vibrancy of the time; the Spirit of God was at work through the Word of God, bringing light and life to people in darkness. Spirit-filled Christians using creativity and their gifts to further the revolution! They were following after the first true reformer and creator.

THE FIRST REFORMER

> *By this the Holy Spirit indicates that the way into the holy places is not yet opened as long as the first section is still standing (which is symbolic for the present age). According to this arrangement, gifts and sacrifices are offered that cannot perfect the conscience of the worshiper, but deal only with food and drink and various washings, regulations for the body imposed until the time of reformation.* (Heb. 9:8-10)

The transition from the Old to New Covenant was the greatest reformation of all time! There's no doubt about it. It was such a revolution against the world, sin and human works for salvation. Jesus appears as the eternal Word of God, the Great High Priest, the King of kings, the first true reformer of the church bringing a better covenant. He flips the world on its head, reforming creation. Christ reformed a temporary redemption by the blood of goats and bulls into an eternal redemption purchased by His own blood. There's never been anything like this and will never be again – there's no need! It is the central climax of the history of the world and of the Bible. But Jesus didn't spend the eternity before His 'putting on flesh' just waiting for His time to come. As we look backwards from the New Testament to Genesis, we can see Jesus, the eternal Word and Son of God, actively involved, speaking and reaching out.

I love this quote from Michael Reeves in his chapter on The Eternal Word, '*For eternity, this Word sounds out, telling us of an uncontainable God, a God of exuberance, of superabundance, an overflowing God, not needy but supremely full and overflowing; a glorious God of grace. Here is a God who loves to give himself.*'[3]

The Word of God became a man and was with the people, the Word who spoke to Abraham, Isaac and Jacob, Moses and Joshua, the prophet Elijah, Daniel and the list goes on… He turned up, and they saw His glory. The Word shows the glory of God, this was displayed on the cross. God who came down to us and humbled Himself to a death on the cross. The glory peculiar to our loving, self-giving God who is abounding in grace and mercy. Him we pursue, our revolutionary God who will be found because of grace, without condition. We seek after the presence of the glory of God, to know Him personally and intimately. To experience and explore how deep is the love of God. By this love for us, the Father sends out the Son to save us.

Through the lens of the Old Testament temple, we see that Jesus is the Great High Priest who is responsible for bringing the sacrifice before God to atone for the sins of the people. Through the cross He brings the great reformation through His own atoning sacrifice. By becoming the sacrifice, He was made sin for us. He who was very God, holy and sinless, was made sin for us. A substitute for our sin, forever. He takes on our sin, we receive His righteousness. Washed by the blood of

---

3 Reeves, M. Ed. Macarthur, J., *High King of Heaven* (Chicago, IL: Moody Publishers, 2018), p.14.

the sacrificial 'lamb' and given a robe of God's righteousness. So, when the Father looks on us He sees the righteousness of His Son through our union with Him.

If the cross were the end of the Jesus story, all He did to save us would have been for nothing. He died and was buried. But there was a revolution over the grave, death had to be beaten. If He hadn't risen from the dead, then it would have meant something devastating about Christ. It would have meant that Jesus wasn't the eternal Word and Son of God sent to save us from our sins. It would have meant that He was a fake Messiah. A revolutionary sham. So, how important is the resurrection of Jesus Christ? It is the critical issue underpinning the gospel about Jesus and the Bible. Only the blood of God's lamb can take away our sin. Christianity is different from all the rest because it boasts an empty grave. Jesus rose from the dead. He appeared to many witnesses. He is alive! And, those who die in Him will follow Him and be raised with Him. Because of the revolution over the grave, we too will have our death-beating revolution like Him and through Him.

The power that raised Jesus from the dead also seated Him at the right hand of power, the trinitarian revolution in action conquering death and rescuing humanity. Hebrews 1:3 says that after making atonement for sin, He sat down at the right hand of the majesty on high as the Son of God. Mission completed! The eternal Son receiving back the glory He had with the Father before the world was made. The risen Son now has supreme authority over all creation. As He raised Christ and seated Him, so we shall be raised and seated with Christ because we are in Him as redeemed co-heirs. How kind, how gracious, how good!

» **Johanna-Ruth Dobschiner**

That very same revolutionary power helps us conquer death as Jesus did, and His light shines even more brightly in the darkest of places. Though we walk through the valley of the shadow of death, we will fear no evil. There are lots of times in our history that seem too evil, hellish and devoid of goodness and love for us to handle. Times like the Holocaust. Has God turned away in such times? No, why do we fear no evil? Because He is with us, and He is still very much at work there.

Guard Tower at Auschwitz

I recently visited Auschwitz for the second time in my life, and the sorrow and human suffering that took place there sunk in much more than the first time I visited. It deeply affected me. I walked in through the gate of death, into the rooms and huts where the enslaved slept, cramped, starving and disease-riddled, treated as less than animals. I touched the blackened walls of the gas chamber where hundreds of thousands died, struggling for air, scratching to escape. I could almost hear the screams of the children. I put my fingers in the holes of the wall where the bullets that killed thousands of innocents hit. The faces of the prisoners that managed to survive just months there have been burned into my mind. It will always be there, I will never forget it. First a Polish army barracks, then a concentration/death camp and lastly an everlasting memorial of humanity without God.

Johanna-Ruth Dobschiner was fourteen years old when the Nazis invaded her country in May 1940, and she witnessed at a young age the invaders in the streets rounding people up for the slaughter. In 1941 anti-Semitism had turned deadly when her own brothers were sent to concentration camps and later returned in ash form back to her parents. 'Hansie' as she was known sought protection as a patient for a time in a Jewish hospital. As she lay in the hospital bed she thought about her Jewish religion in the face of another world war but felt something missing. In the midst of all the suffering and horror God seemed very distant from His people. During December of 1942 she experienced a realisation of the very real presence of God. Her Immanuel (God with us), gave her a glimpse of Himself. This is the grace that got her through the next two terrifying years.

In 1943, her parents were taken to a concentration camp never to be seen again. Later she too would be taken by the army but managed to escape through her quick thinking and resourcefulness, evading death through helping the Germans with translation work and with the sick. The Jewish city hospital where she worked was finally liquidated and she again managed to escape being sent to a death camp through brazen bluff and God's providence over her life. A church pastor gave shelter to Hansie as he did to so many Jews and airmen shot down by the Luftwaffe. He did this as part of his ministry in the North of Holland.

Here were Christians fully taking on the risk of certain death to shelter Hansie and other Jews from the Nazis while sharing the gospel of Jesus. It is beautiful. She began reading the Bible in Dutch and in 1944, in the attic of a safehouse in the South of Holland she realised that Jesus is the promised Messiah. She said, 'I could think no more of God the Father without visualising Jesus Christ.' The Holy Spirit broke through the curtain of her heart with the knowledge that Jesus is alive! At the risk of being made an outcast by the Jewish community in the post-war years she was baptised in the name of the Father, Son and Holy Spirit in November 1944. The following day the reformed minister gave his life to protect those in his care when he was arrested, tortured and shot by the Gestapo.[4]

Johanna's story shows that God doesn't turn away ever. Even in the darkest moments of our history, He is the one who brings light after darkness. The triune God is at work saving souls from hell, bringing freedom to the captives and revolution against tyranny. God overturns our own hearts to bring us back to Him and His truth, so that we love Him more and overflow with grace.

---

[4] Stephens, D. *War and Grace: Short biographies from the World Wars* (Durham, UK: EP Books, 2015), pp. 79-97.

4.
Vive La Revolution

The word revolution comes from the Latin word *revolutio* meaning 'a turnaround'. It usually means a wholesale and sometimes sudden change in government or ruler – when an oppressed population rises up against a tyrannical power. In the American Revolutionary War against the British, the thirteen colonies wanted independence from the British Empire. Various differences with the parliament in England, taxation without representation, the Stamp Act and further escalation gave way to the famous act of dumping a shipment of tea into Boston Harbour.[1] The British government passed laws to punish the Massachusetts colonists, further inflaming the situation towards combat. When the first shot was fired in Lexington, both sides were spoiling for a fight. No one can prove who fired the first shot that it was said could be heard around the world.

---

1   Miller, J. C. *Origins of the American Revolution* (Stanford, CA: Stanford University Press, 1943), pp. 167-8.

General George Washington

In 1776, George Washington was appointed commander-in-chief of the continental army and the war was on! He is considered the beloved hero of the revolution and Father of America, though he knew his fair share of trials and setbacks, betrayal and failure. His decisive victory against the British in 1781 came when his Patriot army trapped the British army in Virginia aided by the French. The British finally surrendered at the battle of Yorktown. In 1781, Great Britain officially recognised the independence of the United States. The revolution was complete, liberty had been won and Washington resigned his commission. Successful revolution against tyranny brings liberty to the oppressed and enslaved.

Sadly not all slaves were freed on the side of the colonists. The British did hold up their end of the deal with plantation slaves who fought for them. Washington himself maintained slaves at his estate until his dying day. It has been proposed that the revolutionary war may have been in part a counter-revolution and the preservation of slavery in the colonies a motivating factor of the war.[2] This is part of the economic context contributing to the uprising. At the time, Britain was passing laws preferring English and Scottish merchants and moving towards abolition of slavery and it was a real financial threat to the colonies who relied on slave cotton labour[3]. The majority of Africans living in the colonies sided with the British in the war. Revolution and counter-revolutions! One thing is sure, there will never be absolutely pure motivations when it comes to a man-made revolution. They are only a shadow of God's revolution against spiritual darkness and the tyranny of death.

As Christians, our revolutionary war isn't against a people or state, but against the slavery of our natures leading to death, the way of the world and the Devil. This revolutionary war was fought and won by Jesus Christ when He died on the bloodstained wooden cross and was resurrected. He was victorious over death and hell. It wasn't fought by an army, weapons and generals. But the revolution isn't over, as long as we're on earth and we wait for Jesus' return. Until that happens, God's church on earth will always be in need of reforming – Vive la Revolution!

We have recently celebrated 500 years of the Reformation, but do we realise that it's a continual reformation? The Church will need constant purifying. My heart and mind will need constant purifying, reforming back to the truth of God's word. We follow our revolutionary leader Jesus Christ, to be truly free and not to be enslaved once again. But this is not freedom to do whatever we want, but liberty from the slavery of the

---

2 Horne, G. *The Counter-Revolution of 1776: Slave Resistance and the Origins of the United States of America* (New York, NY: NYU Press, 2014).

3 *Origins of the American Revolution*, pp. 17-18.

fallen-ness of our nature (the Bible calls it sin). It's often a way soaked with blood and hardship, suffering and glory. We may even have to lay our lives down.

For freedom Christ has set us free; stand firm therefore, and do not submit again to a yoke of slavery. (Gal. 5:1)

In the Apostle Paul's letter to the Galatian church, in chapter 5 he calls them to stay in the revolution. To come back to live in the freedom of God's Spirit, to realign their spiritual identity in line with Christ and trust His word alone. The church in Galatia had been hindered from believing that by grace alone can we be saved. They no longer believed that trusting in Christ alone and having faith in what He did on the cross could make them righteous. They had been tempted to give away their freedom and turn back to 'slavery' and were attempting to include good works to earn their salvation. The Galatian church needed to be continually reforming. This is beautification, we become more beautiful to God through becoming more like His Son. Positive forward movement in the free-way of Jesus.

So, even in the church of the New Testament, reformation was needed to bring them back to the gospel. Paul had to remind them that it is only in Christ and through faith in Him that we can receive righteousness. Cold religion always tries to whisper lies that say, 'Jesus isn't enough'. This is the sinful nature speaking, Paul calls it 'the flesh'. He urges the church to walk by the Spirit of God, the Spirit of freedom and not of slavery. The Spirit of freedom helps us crucify our 'flesh' and our desires that are opposed to the Spirit. Our sinful nature wants to stop us following Christ and living freely. This is the process of dying to ourselves and living for God by the Spirit of God. We need to stand firm, to hold fast against the yoke of slavery. To defend our spiritual freedom.

REVOLUTION MEANS RISK

'Aslan is a lion – the Lion, the great Lion.' 'Ooh' said Susan. 'I'd thought he was a man. Is he quite safe? I shall feel rather nervous about meeting a lion'… 'Safe?' said Mr Beaver … 'Who said anything about safe? Course he isn't safe. But he's good. He's the King, I tell you.' – C.S. Lewis, *The Lion, the Witch and the Wardrobe*

Recently, after an evening of hearing stories and discussing the state of the church in Europe, a good friend whom I admire, asked me very seriously if I was willing to pay the cost of wanting to see the church in Europe grow. That's a difficult question to answer truthfully when someone just comes out and asks you to your face! One doesn't just want to make a hasty reply not fully realising the consequences of saying yes.

Jesus lived a revolutionary life and died a revolutionary's death. Revolution upsets the status quo, and people don't tend to like that, especially if they are enslaved to it. The Bible says that the world hated Jesus, and the logic follows that they will hate us also. As His followers, we follow after and become more like Him, and we're meant to bring the same revolution to the world in darkness. So we can expect the same sort of response from those in darkness.

Jesus never promised an easy time to His followers. To live a life pleasing to God, engaged in the revolution, we shouldn't be surprised by the resistance and persecution we will experience. If we're honest, our natural tendency is to avoid persecution and risk. We want comfort and safety, glory without suffering. But, growth of the church happens under threat as we know from the history of the early church. In the first few centuries, life under Roman rule brought sporadic and state-organised persecution to Christians who were rounded up and brutally put to death. Persecuted Christians used to cry *Maranatha* which means 'Come O Lord' in Aramaic. Risk of death is taken by millions of people every day in countries where it costs to be part of the revolution. What are we willing to risk?

The same friend who gave me that challenge, served his country for many years in the special forces. He tells a story about a daring rescue called Operation Barras. Five British soldiers had been captured in Sierra Leone by an armed gang of thugs and murderers called the West Side Boys. Negotiations to free them had broken down and the decision was made by the British government to rescue the captives and their Sierra Leone liaison officer. The decisive assault by 22 squadron on the West End Boys base took place towards the end of the civil war. A member of the regiment was hit in the side during the operation and put on the helicopter and evacuated from the battlefield. An attempt was made to save him, but the bleeding could not be stopped. Blood washed across the Chinook helicopter floor as the freed soldiers walked on the same helicopter to fly out of danger. They walked through the blood of the fallen soldier who had given his life that they might be freed. They knew that day what their freedom cost someone else.

God the Father willingly sent His only beloved Son to pay the price we could never pay. The Son generously gives Himself to us to receive and God makes His home in us. The gospel is good news about the outgoing loving God giving generously of Himself for the lost. The Father is willing to risk His only Son for our salvation, what are we willing to risk? Our lives? Our wealth and homes?

> *He who supplies seed to the sower and bread for food will supply and multiply your seed for sowing and increase the harvest of your righteousness. You will be enriched in every way to be generous in every way, which through us will produce thanksgiving to God. For the ministry of this service is not only supplying the needs of the saints but is also overflowing in many thanksgivings to God. By their approval of this service, they will glorify God because of your submission flowing from your confession of the gospel of Christ, and the generosity of your contribution for them and for all others, while they long for you and pray for you, because of the surpassing grace of God upon you. Thanks be to God for his inexpressible gift!* (2 Cor. 9:10-14)

The early church were risking their all, every day for the cause of Christ, even their money and comfort. They were denying themselves and giving money away to support the revolution. In this passage, Paul is arranging for a collection from the Corinthian church for needy Christians still living in Jerusalem. He lays out the way Christians should give and the reason why we should give generously and cheerfully. Radical generosity is risky business. We work hard to make money, so we can have comfort and security. And Paul wants us to give it away to help others in need! What about me? I'll be in need then! Being willing to risk our wealth means denying our need of security and trusting in our ability to provide for ourselves. The all too common temptation in the developed world, even for Christians, is to forget about their need for God, 'I can provide for me and live free'.

Jesus didn't hold on to the riches of heaven or equality with God. He humbled Himself by taking the form of a servant – He became a baby born in a stable in a backwater town in Israel and not in the palace in Jerusalem. He humbled Himself even to death as a criminal on the cross. Revolutionary generosity flowing out to the world from the heart of the Father changing everything. To truly take God at His word and trust in His provision we mustn't hold on to our wealth tightly or we're just allowing ourselves to become enslaved again. The giving of financial generosity to 'the saints' flows from our confession of the gospel (what Jesus did), because of what we've received from God! So, as a church we need to confess the gospel in word and also in deed. To live out the gospel overflowing with generosity. *'Whoever will sow generously will also reap generously.'*

REVOLUTIONARY SPIRIT

It all seems rather overwhelming to live as a true follower of Jesus. *Am I being asked to risk my life and give away my well-earned money generously? I want to live in freedom and follow the Spirit, but this is all too much for me!* Well, yes, it is all too much for mere humans, we need power to live like this. But the good news is that our revolutionary leader left in order to send us real help, so the revolution could continue and grow. The Holy Spirit has been sent to give us power and the ability to do all these things that God asks of us through the Bible. Our God is the God of the impossible and we can do all things through Him. He is the strength of our lives, our deep well to draw from. And He has never failed me personally though I often fail Him. How can I access this on-demand help? It is only through prayer!

We endure in prayer, communing with God through His Spirit. Prayer is about knowing God and what He wants for us, and the time we spend with Him in prayer says much about our priorities. The motivation for prayer can be desperation and need, and that isn't a bad thing. The motivation when you're not desperate and needy must be something else though. It's delighting to be with God who delights in us. Prayer has been called 'the key of heaven', and the 'route of godliness'. In prayer, we watch for danger, guard against temptation and we're always ready to praise with thanksgiving for the Lord's goodness. Prayer is the key to unlocking spiritual power in our lives and devotion to God Himself, it's an open door to God. Prayer is how we receive from God and are transformed – where the word and our lives meet!

In chapter 1, we covered what it means to be transformed by the renewal of your mind, being renewed by the Word of God (the truth) and by the Spirit of God. The Spirit is our teacher, He understands the mind of God and we have received Him. He interprets spiritual truths to those who are spiritual (1 Cor. 2:13). So, we can know spiritual truth in a way that those without Him cannot. This is important to remember as we engage with the world around us. We become more and more spiritually mature as we grow in Christ, unlike those who are spiritually dead. So, truth from God is foolishness to the 'dead' world because the truth isn't understood, this includes the gospel, of course. The truth of the cross and of Christ is the wisdom and power of God to those He calls out because they can understand it.

Knowing God by the work of the Spirit through His word has changed me and formed me into the man I am. I now have spiritual fruit in my life from the Holy Spirit, these have changed my natural character and temperament – thank God! I have abilities and gifts that I didn't naturally have. They were endowed to me as He equipped me for every good work – I love Him more as I know Him more and am changed from glory to glory. I am a new man! As lovers of God we experience more of Him in every facet of our lives as we surrender all to Him. He is a God to be known, experienced, pursued and loved.

We share confession in the one Spirit in union together, but in that unity He brings together a diversity of spiritual gifts to the many members of the body. God who is triune loves diversity in unity, so we aren't all the same. God's revolution is made up of diversely gifted people, all serving and working together in harmony under Christ our head! The Bible is clear that these grace gifts are for the common good of the church, not for the individual to profit. All Christians are given spiritual gifts for service in the church – wonderful endowments from God who makes His home in us. This all sounds foolishness to the world but we know they empower us to work for Him. These are revolutionary to us as they are given through second birth, and so we should ask for them and seek to develop them for the Lord.

The revolution in full flow on earth with God's people filled by the Spirit and His power poured out is what we call revival. When revival comes, God's revolution seems more real, heaven seems more real, and certainly more important than this passing world order.[4] In these special times, we're less concerned about our own schemes and our selfishness dissolves as we're more caught up in Christ. In revival, people

---

[4] Carson D. A. *A Call to Spiritual Reformation: Priorities from Paul and His Prayers* (Grand Rapids, MI: Baer Academic, 2006), p. 136.

are concerned with the things of God, they seek to be holy and readily deny themselves. Love abounds, worship flows out of our lives as the revolution heats up. The grace of God works powerfully where mission becomes increasingly more fruitful as a sign of revival. The return of our revolutionary leader seems to come closer. In his letter to the Ephesians, Paul prays that the church in Ephesus might experience revival. We too should pray for revival if we are truly all-in for the revolution. I think for most of the time, we don't want God to rock the boat. We've got everything buttoned down and comfortable, revival would cause change and upset to our routine. So, revival can be inconvenient for us. What are we willing to give to see revival in our land right now?

» John Bunyan

John Bunyan from Bedford, England, was a Christian preacher and writer. You might know of him through his famous allegory of the Christian life entitled *The Pilgrim's Progress*. John Bunyan knew what it cost to be part of the 'Puritan' revolution. The Puritan movement had its roots in the Reformation, which opened access directly to God for everyone through God's Son. The name Puritan was used to describe those who wanted England to be free of Roman Catholic Church interference.[5] The Puritans had a revolutionary and more biblical view of what it meant to be a Christian and there is much we can learn from them. Bunyan was born in 1628 in Elstow, a small village near Bedford. At the age of sixteen he joined the parliamentary Army led by Oliver Cromwell during the English Civil War. After serving for three years he returned to Bedford to work

---

5   Harding R. W. *John Bunyan: His Life and Times* (London, UK: The Epworth Press, 1928), pp. 22-3.

as a tinker (making repairs to pots and pans), which was his father's trade. After his marriage, he joined a protestant group outside the Church of England and became a preacher. He was arrested and spent the next twelve years in jail as he refused to give up preaching the gospel[6].

John Bunyan (1628–1688)

After Cromwell's death, the tolerance which allowed Bunyan the freedom to preach was reversed by the restoration of the monarchy in 1660 with Charles II. It seems incredible to us now, but an act was introduced which meant that preachers had to be ordained by an Anglican bishop; this along with a few other acts meant that it was against the law to hold a non-conformist church service in England! Bunyan was arrested under the Conventicle Act of 1593, which meant it was illegal to attend a church service outside of the Parish church. This gave a lot of power to the bishops and the state church.

The kangaroo court which tried Bunyan took place in 1661 before a group of biased magistrates. He was indicted of having 'devilishly and perniciously abstained from coming to church to hear divine service'. He was sentenced to three months' imprisonment if he didn't agree to attend the parish

---

6   Harrison F. M. *John Bunyan* (London, UK: The Banner of Truth Trust, 1964), pp. 1-9, 149-54.

church and desist from preaching. This all sounds very much like the context in which the Chinese church finds itself today. Bunyan refused to give up on preaching the gospel, and his imprisonment was eventually extended to twelve years, which brought great hardship to his family. John's church supported the family through this period as they were all-in for the revolution with him and standing shoulder to shoulder come what may. Amazingly, the church ordained him as pastor while he was in prison! Bunyan was released in 1672 and immediately obtained a licence to preach under the declaration of indulgence.

During his time as His Majesty's guest he wrote his first book, a spiritual autobiography called *Grace abounding to the Chief of Sinners* and later began his most famous work. *The Pilgrim's Progress* became one of the most published works in the English language. In his dark cold dungeon cell, he had time to pray and think and dream. Perhaps writing was an escape from the harshness he had to endure. But, like saints before him, the prison could not hold him captive. He ministers to the world, calling sinners to salvation in Jesus and for Christians to stay the course through the journey. He describes his dream from which the book emerged:

> *And thus it was: I, writing of the way and race of saints in this our Gospel-day, fell suddenly into an Allegory about their journey, and the way to glory.*

Through his ordeal, Bunyan would have felt rejected, downtrodden and an outcast from his society. He'd have felt like an exile in his own land with the government and law opposing him and his church. *Pilgrim's Progress* has been said to be a portrait of Bunyan's life. A pilgrim, journeying through this world to heaven. In his changing circumstances, especially during his years at Bedford prison, the Lord was ever present and unchanging. The revolutionary way is a way of newness, of risk and suffering. It is a well-worn way for all the race of saints who are journeying to glory following after Jesus.

5.
The Father of Revolutions

God doesn't ever change, and because He doesn't change, the world must change and conform to His will as its creator. God is always the one who is bringing revolution for His glory and for the sake of His Church, working out His divine plan for the world. He is the father of revolution but doesn't reform Himself. This is what He says about Himself in Malachi 3:6:

> *For I the LORD do not change; therefore you, O children of Jacob, are not consumed.*

We're always changing as societies and communities of people. The world changes, governments and empires change. We change our minds and how we feel a hundred times a day! We tend to turn this way and that, we struggle to keep our hearts warm and keep faith with our God. The good news about our God's consistency is that He keeps His promises and His word, and His nature is the same today as 6,000 years ago. He still keeps promises He made with Abraham when He called him from Haran to a promised land. And He is still gracious, merciful and slow to anger. This is why Abraham's offspring are not consumed for turning away and worshipping other gods. Abraham's descendants broke their union with their God, they broke the covenant over and over. God doesn't ever change, but we do. This is why He needs to be constantly reforming us, His covenant people. He is the one who reforms His church at His time and in His way. He brings the revolution which causes positive change by drawing us closer to Him, and He accomplishes His will. Man-made revolutions in the church result in damage to the church and a falling away, having the opposite effect.

At the tower of Babel, God 'came down' and brought confusion on all humanity through the introduction of different languages, dispersing humanity across the face of the earth rather than their being united in one tribe. He did this to stop them in their tracks as they desired glory for themselves rather than glorifying their creator. It was an attempt by

The Tower of Babel

humanity to become equal with God. So, the Godhead came to reform society and community for our good and His glory. Now, through Christ, we are united together once again in Him by His Spirit with a common spiritual language, and our aim is for Him and His kingdom. Each person fitting together like bricks to make God's holy tower.

God the Father has been reforming His creation since the Fall, all with the aim of restoring creation back to Himself through His called-out people, beginning with Abraham. Abraham was the first significant step to restoring Eden. The establishing of the covenant and promises, building through Genesis. In the great world-wide flood, the Lord reformed humanity and the world through the judgment of the flood. The Bible says that such was the evil on the earth that God pressed the reset button on creation around a faithful family preserved through the ark of salvation. This is a wonderful picture of Christ. The faithful were saved inside the ark, and we are in Christ, who is our salvation, to save us from God's coming judgment on the world. Let's remember that this world is God's creation. We are not our own, we are created by Him and for Him. Yet, we want to be our own gods. Left to that end, we descend into chaos and evil.

In Genesis 15, God promised, through His covenant to Abraham, that Abraham's descendants would be as numerous as the stars in the sky but would also be enslaved in Egypt where they would grow up into a nation. He also said that in the right time He would judge the Egyptians and free His people, eventually leading them to the land promised to Abraham. Moses was God's man, sent to lead the revolution against the Egyptians to freedom and their inheritance. God is building up His called-out people and bringing them to His promised place to be His people. What seems like a negative thing to happen, God means for their good and to achieve His pre-set plan. Firstly, Egypt saved them from hunger, then provided shelter so the people could grow and multiply over a couple of hundred years. Then at the right time, they emerged a mighty nation ready to inhabit the promised land and to clear out the Canaanites and other inhabitants, and laws are given under the covenant for the nation. God isn't afraid to use any means to achieve His purposes even if it looks like He is throwing everything up in the air and then putting it all back together. With the exile of the Jews to Babylon, they were enslaved and carried off so He might redeem them once again to Himself and restore them back to the land of their inheritance ready for the coming of the promised Messiah. These are the promises of God, and God keeps His promises.

God's covenant with Abraham and His children is like a marriage union. There are promises to keep, although God underwrites their part because they keep breaking them. This is the grace of God, and for us Jesus underwrites our part as we are grafted into the covenant. Christ fulfils the law for us that we might believe and be justified by faith, as was Abraham. In Galatians 3:26-9, Paul says, *'for in Christ Jesus you are all sons of God, through faith. For as many of you as were baptized into Christ have put on Christ. There is neither Jew nor Greek, there is neither slave nor free, there is no male and female, for you are all one in Christ Jesus. And if you are Christ's, then you are Abraham's offspring, heirs according to promise'.* God is progressively reforming His covenant.

The author of creation has every right to progressively reform His creation, just like a potter with a lump of clay. It's a process of shaping and reshaping until there's a finished article fit for firing and then purpose. God in His infinite wisdom creates a world and a people in His own image to inhabit it so He would be their God, knowing that they would break union and disobey Him. He created us to be free, only for us to fall under the power of sin and in need of saving from God's justice. He knew in the beginning He would be reforming His creation because He is all-knowing and sovereign over creation, but He still made things the way He did. It's not that the all-knowing, sovereign God didn't know what would happen in the garden of Eden. Yet He allowed Satan to tempt Adam and Eve to disobey Him and eat the forbidden fruit, which meant that they would eventually die as this is the fruit of sin. We see in that first marriage blueprint a figure of Christ and His church. God in creation is teaching us of His plan for our union with His Son through His suffering on the cross.[1] In Genesis 2, God created man and then woman from man. God caused a strange deep sleep to fall on Adam, who is then wounded and part of himself is removed to give life to Eve. He created the woman out of Adam's body and life, to become one flesh with Adam in union. In the same way, Christ the last Adam was wounded in His side and gave of Himself from His body and life for the church on the cross, and they became one in union. Paul calls this a profound mystery in Ephesians 5:32.

If we see this life as our final destination and this time as our time, then this point of predestination will seem a bit 'far out'. But, if we see this life as preparation for death where we will be with God for infinitely more time, then it makes sense. Being a disciple in this life on earth is a time to learn how to follow Jesus Christ, to die to our old self and be alive to God to

---

1   Calvin. J. *Institutes of the Christian Religion* (New York, NY: Collins, 1975 edition), pp.172-5.

live our new life in Christ forever! This is a revolutionary way of seeing the world and we can only see it if we really see God as God! One day Jesus will return to judge the world and bring an end to this age, bringing cleansing and healing to the earth God's people will inherit.

» Dietrich Bonhoeffer

From our human point of view, you could ask, 'If he is sovereign, why did God allow Hitler to become leader of the Nazi party and begin his conquest of Europe in World War II?' The Nazis were responsible for the systematic murder of 17 million people, 6.9 million of them Jews. As we know from the story of Johanna-Ruth Dobschiner, there are little glimmers of light in the darkness. God doesn't abandon us in the darkest pages of human history. Even in Nazi Germany there was a resistance against the evil and God had His people there to resist evil and darkness.

Dietrich Bonhoeffer (1906–1945)

Dietrich Bonhoeffer was a German Lutheran pastor and theologian who was active in the German resistance to the policies of Hitler and Nazism. It is important that as Christians

The Father of Revolutions

we do obey the law and submit to government authority as God has placed them there for law and order. However, as with the Nazis, there are times when governments and leaders commit acts of evil against God and man, and we must stand against such governments and powers. God's wrath will be revealed and He will wipe away evil from the land.

Bonhoeffer didn't run away from the tyranny taking over Europe, he was in the resistance against evil. He went to New York to sit out the war as many German theologians did at the time, but he couldn't stay there and promptly returned to Germany. He counted the cost of following Christ and opposed Nazism from within Nazi Germany. Knowing the risk to his life, he put himself in harm's way. In 1936, he wrote *The Cost of Discipleship*, for he believed without a doubt that discipleship was costly.

As part of the Valkyrie plot to blow up Hitler, Bonhoeffer 'the wartime spy' and others in the resistance had concluded that the assassination attempt must be attempted at any cost.[2] Even if the attempt failed, it had to be done by the German resistance in full view of the world. We know that this attempt ultimately failed, but they weren't playing at stopping Hitler, they were all-in. With very high stakes, they all knew the option of sitting passively and watching on wasn't for them. They couldn't just sit by doing nothing to try to stop the madness.

Silence in the face of evil is itself evil: God will not hold us guiltless. Not to speak is to speak. Not to act is to act. – Dietrich Bonhoeffer

In April 1945, Bonhoeffer the revolutionary was hanged by the Nazis for standing up against evil and tyranny. He followed

---

[2] Metaxis. E. *Bonhoeffer: Pastor, Martyr, Prophet, Spy* (Nashville, TN: Thomas Nelson, 2010), pp. 475-80.

his saviour to the gallows. He could do this because his view was that death was merely the beginning of the rest of his life. He preached the gospel to other political prisoners during his time in various places right up to the last moment. Five months later and the war would be over. God in His wisdom allowed Hitler to take power and inflame a nation, but God also enabled the allied nations to stand against and defeat this great evil against all odds.

Bonhoeffer was following his God. God does act in the face of an evil committed against Him and His people. He isn't watching passively on, unable to act. We see this so clearly in the gospel. In love, the Father sends out His Son to lead a revolution against death and hell to redeem us back to Himself. This is what the flow of the Bible is about and the purpose of our having it. The whole point of the Bible is that we see Jesus! This is the orthodox view of the early church, the Reformers and Puritans. The Bible isn't some randomly arranged books by different authors in chronological order. The author is God and He used faithful followers to write and publish His word. So, God speaks through the Bible and we can read it as a complete book. It is our supreme authority and we are to trust it and believe on it to the very end. He has promised to come back and renew all things to be like it was in the beginning.

REFORMING EDEN

Then the angel showed me the river of the water of life, bright as crystal, flowing from the throne of God and of the Lamb through the middle of the street of the city; also, on either side of the river, the tree of life with its twelve kinds of fruit, yielding its fruit each month. The leaves of the tree were for the healing of the nations. (Rev. 22:1-2)

Jonathan Edwards (1703 – 1758)

Let's look to the end of the Bible, how does the story end? In the book of Revelation, there is a new creation with the city of God and at its centre the lamb who is outflowing with light and life, He is the radiance of God's glory. There'll be no need for sun, for He will be the source of light. The light is the glory of God that has driven out the darkness. From Him, glory and love radiate outwards, teaching us of a God who doesn't need to receive but to give out. His glory is radiating, self-giving and loving. And there is the city called the New Jerusalem with Jesus at its centre, (who is the glory of His Father's brightness and humble as a lamb) with the river of the water of life springing from the throne of God and Jesus. What an incredible image! Can you imagine it? Here we can see the triune God in His full splendour in a place where His presence dwells. Jonathan Edwards, an American revolutionary, describes it as, *'The Son of God, who is the brightness of the Father's glory, appears there in the fullness of his glory, without that garb of outward meanness in which he appeared in this world. The Holy Ghost shall there be poured forth with perfect richness and sweetness, as a pure river of the water of life, clear as crystal, proceeding out of the throne of God and of the Lamb'.*[3]

---

3   Edwards. J. 'Heaven: A World of Love'. www.uniontheology.org.

The river of living waters theme runs through the Bible. We know that Jesus is the spring of life, as He describes Himself in John chapter 4. It says, whoever drinks of the water He gives, shall never thirst again. The water Jesus gives will become in the drinker, a spring of water welling up to eternal life. The Holy Spirit being poured out in our hearts, a fountain of eternal life. All springs flowing together like a big river.

There is another place in the Bible where we see the river of life. In Ezekiel chapter 47, his vision of the river of life flowing from out of the sanctuary of the temple is hugely significant. It looks past the restoration of Jerusalem after the exile to Babylon, to a better Jerusalem prophesied in Revelation chapter 22. In Ezekiel's vision, as in Revelation, the river of life is flowing out from Jesus – the temple here is symbolic for the Christ who would be killed and then resurrected after three days. Ezekiel's river flows east from the mercy seat, from under the temple into the Dead Sea, making it fresh once again and bringing life to it. This obviously hasn't happened, as it is symbolic language that teaches us about the significance of the temple. It points to how Jesus takes the place of the temple as the sacrificial atonement and great High Priest. He gives us living water, making what was dead come alive! The river of life is flowing from Eden through history and on into the new creation and forever. It never stops flowing, because Christ is life and we are in Him.

The river of the water of life, the tree of life on either side, bearing fruit with leaves that heal the nations. There are obvious parallels with Eden here as told in Genesis: a tree of life, garden and river running out of Eden. In Genesis 3, God gives the promise of Christ after the curse of the Fall (Eden lost) – it was a place of delight for people to enjoy God and

His creation. However, through the curse, love and delight were replaced with suffering, pain and hardship. A life without God. But now our revolutionary leader who has crushed the enemy's head has reversed the curse for all those in Him. He brings a new creation for us. So, at the end of time, it will be like it was in the beginning. Although, this isn't Eden merely restored for us, for this is a better Eden, because of the second Adam, Jesus. Jesus is better than Adam and head of the new creation. There'll be no serpent and no forbidden tree, only the tree of life. God's revolution is over, Jesus has won. This time, there isn't a garden with only a husband and wife, but a city full of the glory of God and multitudes of His gathered people from the nations.

He gives us a place with Him, a world of love and delight for God's people to live with Him for ever. We who live in the city of man are to look up to the city of God, the city of love. The new Jerusalem is a beautiful city full of life and full of the church, the full number of those who have been saved by Jesus. They will have spiritual bodies.[4] Perfect and eternal like His. The Church will be in a perfected state there, no longer militant. The end has come, there is eternal glorious victory and now no need for revolution, only perfection. There the Holy Spirit is more abundantly given to the Church, poured out in divine love in the hearts of all inhabitants. They have perfect communion with the Holy Spirit producing perfect love. As Jonathan Edwards puts it, this is a world of love because God Himself lives there and He is divine love.[5]

This is our very real hope of eternity with God, and it should fill our hearts with gladness and love for Him. Being with our

---

4 Reeves. M. *Christ our Life* (Milton Keynes: Paternoster, 2014), p. 103.
5 Edwards. J. 'Heaven: A World of Love'.

God in heaven, God the Father, God the Son and God the Spirit, united as one. It is too much for me to get my head around, this river of love and delight. He is there at the end of time, and He is there before it, unchanging. He is the same today as He was ten thousand years ago. He is the revolutionary God of love. Reforming creation, reviving His church, giving us life and renewing us. And we are created to be like Him, like Jesus.

Conclusion

This truth is incendiary, it ignites reformation and movements among God's people. I wrote this book as a call to the revolution. Primarily, for friends and church members to mobilise them to grow in their faith and make disciples. To call churches to reformation, to come back to the old paths laid down by the Reformers and Puritans. To see more people become effective disciples of Jesus in the world. He sends us out into the world as His Father sent Him to share His life with us. We follow Jesus to the place of rejection, joining Him there in mission. He is with us in this task and for us, so who can be against us (Rom. 8:31)? God who didn't spare His own Son, but lovingly sent Him into the worst. We follow Him to the place of rejection, joining Him who has been sent on mission. The same God will help and equip us, He will give us all things necessary for our mission. Why wouldn't He? And why wouldn't we believe Him?

If you identify yourself as a Christian, then this is for you as a child of God and not just for your church leaders. When

Jesus saves you, you are set free to live and you join the Jesus revolution. You are called to be 'all-in'. It does put you at odds with the world and that's the cost. So, are you willing to be all-in, on Jesus' side? To carry your cross and keep dying to your old nature? Are you willing to join the ranks of those described below? Those of whom the world was not worthy. They are our witnesses, and what will you do? I'll leave you with this great challenge from the book of Hebrews:

For time would fail me to tell of Gideon, Barak, Samson, Jephthah, of David and Samuel and the prophets – who through faith conquered kingdoms, enforced justice, obtained promises, stopped the mouths of lions, quenched the power of fire, escaped the edge of the sword, were made strong out of weakness, became mighty in war, put foreign armies to flight. Women received back their dead by resurrection. Some were tortured, refusing to accept release, so that they might rise again to a better life. Others suffered mocking and flogging, and even chains and imprisonment. They were stoned, they were sawn in two, they were killed with the sword. They went about in skins of sheep and goats, destitute, afflicted, mistreated–of whom the world was not worthy – wandering about in deserts and mountains, and in dens and caves of the earth. (Heb. 11:32-38)

Revolutionaries following after their revolutionary God.

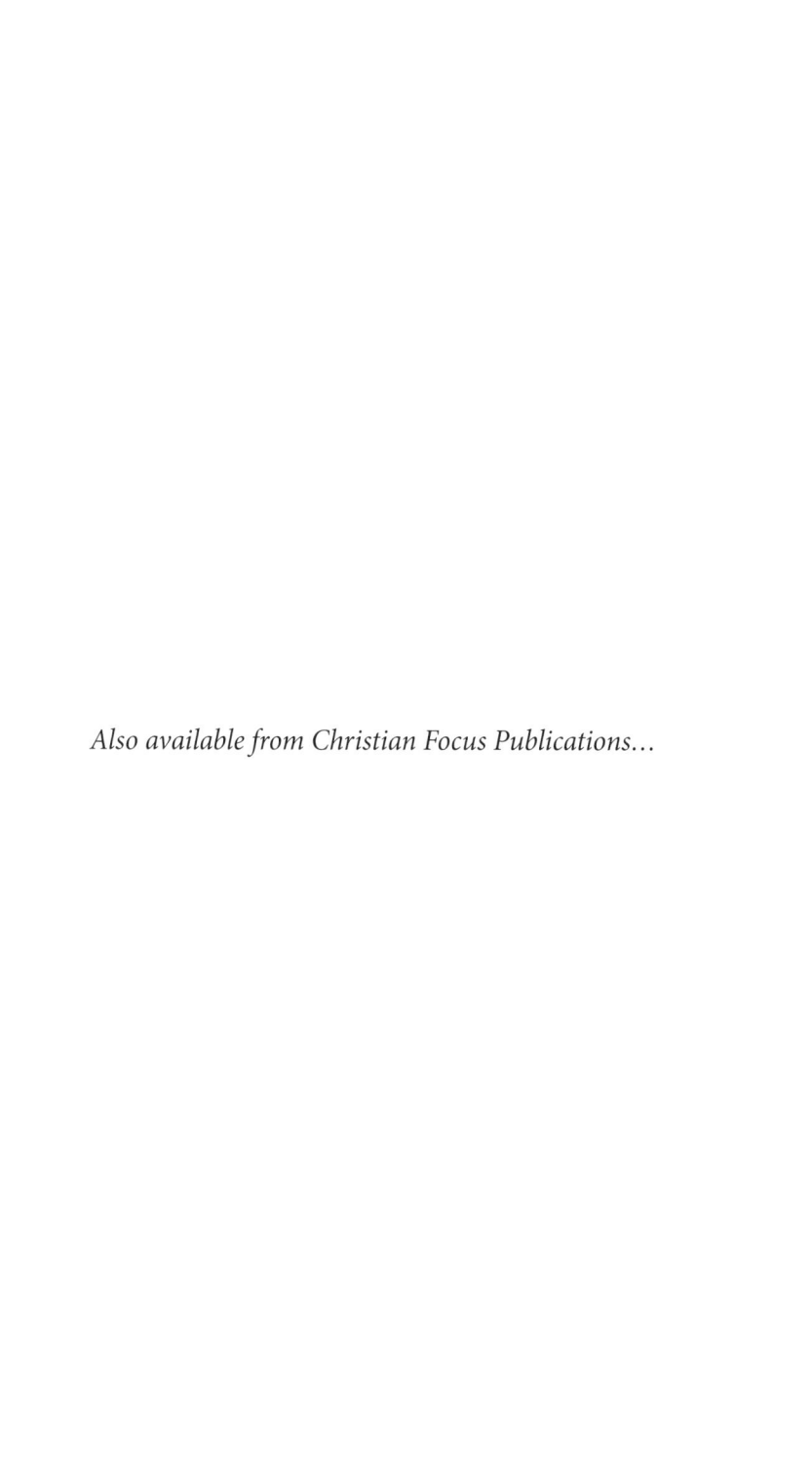

Also available from Christian Focus Publications…

Steve Nation

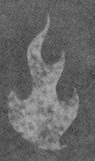

A Call to Extraordinary Prayer

Recharging your Prayer Life through the Book of Acts

A Call to Extraordinary Prayer

Recharging your Prayer Life through the Book of Acts

STEVE NATION

The book of Acts shows the importance of the link between the ministry of the Word and prayer. It teaches us that a distinguishing mark of a Christian and of a truly Biblical church is that they pray. *A Call to Extraordinary Prayer* is a call to pray with a passion, urgency, and hope.

A Call to Extraordinary Prayer *is part study of prayer in Acts, and part rally cry to the church gathered to pray. Read it and you will be greatly encouraged and motivated to pray because we pray to our great God, good and powerful, and the sovereign overseer of our lives. Read it and you will most likely be rebuked as the spotlight is shone on your own prayer life. The church gathered is the church praying: is that true of us?*

Jenny Salt
Dean of Students, Sydney Missionary and Bible College, Sydney

... biblical, readable and well-illustrated. The relationship of Word and prayer must be restored in our lives and churches.

D. Eryl Davies
Elder, Heath Evangelical Church, Cardiff & Consulting Editor, Evangelical Magazine

978-1-5271-0089-3

JOSH MOODY

How the Bible Can Change Your Life

ANSWERS TO THE TEN MOST COMMON
QUESTIONS ABOUT THE BIBLE

How the Bible Can Change Your Life

Answers to the Ten Most Common Questions about the Bible

Josh Moody

Christians are Bible people. We believe that God speaks to us through His inspired Word. And yet many Christians and churches don't actually open their Bibles. Josh Moody asks the question: Why should I read the Bible?

Following on from *How Church Can Change Your Life,* Moody tackles the next great challenge for contemporary Christians: faith in and practice of the Bible, answering 10 of the most common questions about the Bible:

Is the Bible True?
Is the Bible Relevant?
Is the Bible Interesting?
Is the Bible Authoritative?
How Do You Read the Bible?
When Do You Read the Bible?
Does it Matter if We Use the Bible in Church?
Does the Bible Make You Stupid?
Does the Bible Prevent a Tolerant Society?

A powerful blend of penetrating argument and practical application, this is a God–centred challenge to prevailing contemporary attitudes. It will send you back to the Bible with renewed confidence and fresh expectation.

David Jackman
Past President, The Proclamation Trust, London

978-1-5271-0151-7

Christian Focus Publications

Our mission statement –

STAYING FAITHFUL

In dependence upon God we seek to impact the world through literature faithful to His infallible Word, the Bible. Our aim is to ensure that the Lord Jesus Christ is presented as the only hope to obtain forgiveness of sin, live a useful life and look forward to heaven with Him.

Our books are published in four imprints:

CHRISTIAN FOCUS

Popular works including biographies, commentaries, basic doctrine and Christian living.

CHRISTIAN HERITAGE

Books representing some of the best material from the rich heritage of the church.

MENTOR

Books written at a level suitable for Bible College and seminary students, pastors, and other serious readers. The imprint includes commentaries, doctrinal studies, examination of current issues and church history.

CF4•K

Children's books for quality Bible teaching and for all age groups: Sunday school curriculum, puzzle and activity books; personal and family devotional titles, biographies and inspirational stories – because you are never too young to know Jesus!

Christian Focus Publications Ltd,
Geanies House, Fearn, Ross-shire,
IV20 1TW, Scotland, United Kingdom.
www.christianfocus.com
blog.christianfocus.com